Why I Didn't and Why You Shouldn't Commit Suicide

Why I Didn't and Why You Shouldn't Commit Suicide

Dr. Roy E. Gaiter Sr.

Why I Didn't and Why You Shouldn't Commit Suicide
Roy E. Gaiter Sr.

All rights reserved. No part of this publication may be reproduced, stored in retrieval system or transmitted in any form by any means, electronic, mechanical, photocopy, recording or otherwise, without the prior permission of the publisher, except as provided by USA copyright law.

© Copyright Dr. Roy E. Gaiter Sr. 2017
All right reserved

ISBN-13: 9781979529167
ISBN-10: 1979529167

Preface

When I first started writing this book I said to myself, "If I can turn only one person from suicide then it would be worth it." But this issue is so important, why wish for one. What I really want is for this book to influence thousands.

It is short by design, for it is not likely that a person wants to read a book, and much less a large volume considering their desperate situation about life.

The goal of this book is simple, to turn someone away from committing suicide. Therefore, the title invites the reader into the life of one who experienced impulses of suicide, but who did not succumb to them.

In the pages of this book there are twelve reasons "why I didn't and why you shouldn't" end your life. The lives of famous people, leaders, celebrities, Shakespearian writing, biblical narratives, military personal, veterans, and more are considered within the text.

This work does not prescribe medicine nor seek to take the place of any medical or professional health provider. Therefore, it is limited in addressing Post Traumatic Stress. Instead what it seeks to do is encourage alternatives to suicide, and appeal to the common appreciation of life.

I want to acknowledge those serving actively in the military and the previous service of veterans. As an organization you have a duty to serve and protect others with your lives. My optimism is that the duty of this book will appeal, inspire, and serve to avoid—suicide.

Table of Contents

One	"I didn't because suicide is not worth my life"	1
Two	"I didn't because I was someone's baby with relatives"	11
Three	"I didn't because you were always there"	17
Four	"I didn't because I didn't want to"	25
Five	"I didn't because there were other options"	31
Six	"I didn't because other's didn't"	39
Seven	"I didn't because my pockets were empty"	45
Eight	"I didn't because I was only down, not defeated"	55
Nine	"I didn't because I knew somebody loved me"	61
Ten	"I didn't because there were many uncertainties"	67
Eleven	"I didn't because troubles have benefits"	73
Twelve	"I didn't because I was not alone"	79

Reference List · 87
About the Author · 91

One

"I DIDN'T BECAUSE SUICIDE IS NOT WORTH MY LIFE"

Misguided Statement

Albert Camus wrote this misguided statement in "*The Myth of Sisyphus and Other Essays,*" "There is but one truly serious philosophical problem, and that is suicide. Judging whether life is or is not worth living amounts to answering the fundamental question of philosophy." (Camus p. 3)

In Greek mythology Sisyphus is forced to roll a large stone to the top of a hill. The stone rolls back down the hill and Sisyphus has to roll the stone up the hill again. It is repeated over and over again until it becomes an exercise in futility.

What is meant by Camus statement is, once someone has discovered that life has no meaning, an absurdity; then life is not worth living, suicide becomes the only logical grim problem or question to answer.

Really! "*Only* suicide is left to be answered and no other," says Ravi Zacharias. Unfortunately for many that is the circumstance.

Dr. Roy E. Gaiter Sr.

The Stanford Encyclopedia of Philosophy on *Camus* in a 2012 Internet edition challenges Camus statement on suicide when it says, "that suicide is neither a "problem" nor a "question," but an act" ("Albert Camus" The Stanford Encyclopedia of Philosophy (Spring 2012 Edition).

Sadly it is the last act for some. Therefore, understanding why your life is *worth* living would be a more important consideration. And the question of where does *worth* and *meaning* come from, is a good place to start. For if life has meaning, then there would be no need to consider suicide, ever.

Consider this scenario: what if when life feels so intolerable, you think you are worthless and life meaningless; and then you discover that those feelings are not equivalent to being worthless? Even better, what if you discovered that worthlessness and meaninglessness as applied to people does not exist?

Where Does Worth Come From?

If we are to understand worth and meaning, then we need to begin with understanding. It is believed that our understanding of worth or meaning comes from our past, our culture, our experiences, etc.

In a 2009 abstract found in the *National Institutes of Health* entitled "*Alone and without purpose: Life loses meaning following social exclusion,*" Meaning is said to come in this manner, "In principle people could find meaning in communing with nature or divinity, engaging in philosophical or religious contemplation, pursuing scientific or artistic technological innovation or other potentially solitary pursuits." (Tyler F. Stillman, Roy F. Baumeister, Nathaniel M. Lambert, A. Will Crescioni, C. Nathan DeWall, and Frank D. Fincham, 2009)

Four Needs For Meaning Human

In the same article, reference is made to four human needs for meaning.

> "On a broad array of topics including love, work, religion, culture, suicide, and parenthood, Baumeister (1991) concluded that the human experience is shaped by four needs for meaning, 1) a sense of purpose . . . relating to future outcomes; 2) people desire feelings of *efficacy* . . . they [need the ability to] make a difference in some important way; 3) people want to view their actions as having positive *value* or as being morally justified; 4) people want a sense of *positive self-worth*. They seek ways of establishing that they are individuals with desirable traits. (Tyler F. Stillman, Roy F. Baumeister, Nathaniel M. Lambert, A. Will Crescioni, C. Nathan DeWall, and Frank D. Fincham, 2009)

After considering all these pursuits and needs that people have, it is safe to say that people have an inclination to reverence something or someone. This reverence may not be to a deity, but it is reverence. It could be money. It could be sex. It could be learning. It could be our own selves. People worship sticks and stones, animals, houses, cars, and universal stellar bodies.

With the exception of God, the others share little about our worth and little or nothing about our purpose. They simply say to what we pay attention to, not our purpose. Therefore, we need to take another look.

Another Look at Where Worth Comes From

Knowledge of our origins establishes confidence, hope and provides a *foundation* to support us through the difficult times of our lives. In fact how we began is important to our ending. Foundations are needed for stability so that buildings will not fall. People also need foundations to prevent falling. Friends and things are helpful, but they can and often will fail us. Therefore worth must come from a foundational source outside of us.

While visiting Ohio State University, Ravi Zacharias a notable speaker came across America's post-modernist architect building which had no purpose, with a stairway that led to nowhere, and with pillars that joined nothing. Ravi good-humoredly asked, about the architect, "Did he do the same with the foundation?" (Zacharias, 2014)

Post-modernist architect building

A Foundation of Meaning

There are two main opposing sources for the foundation and origin of human beings. One is *evolution*. The idea of this theory is that life started from a simple form by *chance* and developed into a more complex form as it is today. This took allegedly millions of years, the fittest of these forms according to the theory "naturally survived" and prevailed over weaker forms. Charles Darwin laid the foundation for this theory.

The problem with evolution is that its "parent" is assumed to be chance. Furthermore if it is to continue to thrive, devotees must keep constant vigilance at the gym so that they can be the fittest of all forms to survive everybody else, being envious and detestable of others, prideful and glowing over themselves. Nothing is wrong with being healthy, but living in this way, can make a person very unpleasant and very tired.

The other is *creation* from scripture. There are four things that scripture reveals about worth and meaning:

First meaning is "bestowed" to humans, giving them *purpose and relating our present events to future outcomes. "For I know the plans I have for you," declares the LORD, "plans to prosper you and not to harm you, plans to give you hope and a future Jeremiah 29: 11."* Scripture also says this about mankind, *"And God said, Let us make man in our image, after our likeness: (Genesis 1:26).*

To be *made* is purposeful. This is not a bang, an accident or chance. We are *made* in the image of God therefore we are to be *reflectors* of that image in the present and the future.

Second, the need of efficacy or abilities are spoken of in scripture in this manner,

> *"And let them have dominion over the fish of the sea, and over the fowl of the air, and over the cattle, and over all the earth, and over*

every creeping thing that creepeth upon the earth . . . And God blessed them, and God said unto them, Be fruitful, and multiply, and replenish the earth, and subdue it: and have dominion over the fish of the sea, and over the fowl of the air, and over every living thing that moveth upon the earth" (Genesis 1:26, 28).

There can be no doubt, that of all the creatures made, *only* humans have dominion over all other creatures. Note: there is a distinction here. This is *not* dominion over ones neighbors it is over other creatures. Moreover, only humans have high intellectual abilities, to construct a space station, build computers, automobiles and to be caretakers of the earth.

Third, the need of having positive moral value is contained in the words, *"God said, Let us make man in our image, after our likeness: (Genesis 1:26).* Humans have a moral conscience as their moral Maker. Therefore the invention of the polygraph test is somewhat effective in its application to moral truthfulness or falsehood. Additionally honor, *character* and *integrity* are important words, to both military and non-military individuals, for we all are made in the image of God.

Fourth, the need of sensing their worth is seen in that humans were made different from the rest of creation, and given *intelligence* and *awareness* of their worth to honor their Maker. *"And God saw every thing that he had made, and, behold, it was very good (Genesis 1:21).*

A Need For Relationship

There is a need for man to have relationships. Not only with the rest of the creation but also with the Maker. "The formation and maintenance of positive close relationships can aptly be characterized as one of the primary motivations for human beings". (Tyler F. Stillman, Roy F. Baumeister, Nathaniel M. Lambert, A. Will Crescioni, C. Nathan DeWall, and Frank D. Fincham, 2009).

Life Lesson One: There is no need to look for meaning for your life; you are already made with meaning.

Connectedness and relationship to the Maker is necessary to the foundation and meaning of our existence to insure we are not just a cosmic accident. Unlike rocks, wind and water humans have needs for connection. More importantly the Maker desires to have a relationship with us as well.

Unfailing Love

When a child has done something wrong parents don't approve of the wrong, but the love for the child is maintained. So it is with our Maker. We are still loved. So if we love our children, when they make mistakes, our Maker loves us even more. In addition forgiveness is graciously available without cost. When we accept forgiveness it means that whatever others have done to us, or whatever we have done to ourselves, we must let it go.

So there are two questions that need to be answered. The first is, "Does my Maker love me? If the answer is yes, then that means you know you are of great worth. We have already showed that you were made with purpose. The second is; Am I willing to give my life to my Maker.

Someone Took Our Place

Larnelle Harris sings a song titled *"Were It Not For Grace"*. It tells of the shortness of time we have to live our lives which is already measured for us. The lyrics speak of lingering memories of a past painful life, with unsuccessful methods to obtain peace. They tell of our powerlessness to do anything about worsening shortcomings. The song mentions battles, struggles and running in the race of life, but losing. Then grace shows up through a person who takes our place. It is our Maker who walks in our shoes and dying in our behalf, going "the final mile between heaven and us so we would not be lost." "But you, Lord, are a shield around me, my glory, the One who lifts my head high." (Psalms 3:3 NIV)

That's why problems so deeply rooted and hurtful belong to our Maker, the foundation of our worth. Every time we feel we have run out of choices, grace will seek to take our place. And because of grace the focus shifts from "me" to the One who took my place. I discovered suicide was not *worth* my life. That's why I didn't, and that's why you shouldn't commit suicide.

*"When you feel like giving up, just remember
the reason you held on for so long"*

-U<small>NKNOWN</small>

Two

"I didn't because I was someone's baby with relatives"

Babies Don't Commit Suicide

Let us put aside the reasons for suicide for a moment and ask a simple question: How old are you? Really, how old are you? Have you noticed babies do not commit suicide? Why is that so? Is it because they have so little life experiences? Is it because a baby's development has not run its course? Is it because a baby does not understand from cause to consequences, the impact of actions, and with thoughts, come a flood of feelings, about those thoughts?

I was only twenty years old when the notion of suicide became a consideration that I contemplated. Some would say at that age I was just a baby. And I had not lived long enough to do such a thing. Furthermore, they would ask, what about your ambitions, aspirations, and living for a purpose.

The truth is I was a normal twenty year old, and the future seemed so far away. The present was the only thing that was important. I'll share my story later in the book.

It is likely as you read this short book you are not a baby. Also, chances are you are not that old. The notion of suicide as a remedy to adverse experiences, unpleasant emotions, physical abnormalities, or disappointing relationships need not be the end of your life. There is still some growing to do.

According to an ancient inspired book, when we live to be three score and ten years (70 years of age) we are doing well. I have personally met and have taken pictures with a woman who was approaching 108 years of age. Good or bad she had almost 108 years of experiences.

You don't remember when you were a newborn baby. But your birth experience was one of the most difficult experiences you've ever gone through. And guess what, you made it through. We are really talking about immaturity here.

Before you were a newborn you went through some incredible stuff.

> "The human body is made of 11 important organ systems, including the circulatory, respiratory, digestive, excretory, nervous and endocrine systems. They also include the immune, integumentary, skeletal, muscle and reproductive systems. The systems work together to maintain a functioning human body." (Google snippet extracted from web page, "what are the systems of the human body")

Lungs had to be formed, eyes, bones, blood, and the wiring of a nervous system. Before birth, everything needed to be functional, all in nine months. This does not include living in amniotic fluid and the amazing journey inside the mother to the actual birth.

Why I Didn't and Why You Shouldn't Commit Suicide

As a newborn you were the center of attention to nurses, doctors, and the entire medical staff. But it was your mother and father who experienced the most joy.

In rare occasions, the biological parents may not be known. But it does not change the fact that you are still someone's baby, and you will be their baby for life.

Relatives and Relationships

Good relationships are important to development and connecting with others living in the social environment; therefore, before you came there were sisters and brothers perhaps already waiting for your arrival. You already had grandfathers and grandmothers. You probably had or will have nieces, nephews, uncles, aunts, and cousins. And if you are grown, perhaps you may have a spouse and even children of your own.

Relationships in general have far more potential for love rather than hatred. Unfortunately some people have unresolved family relationships. These unresolved relationships could become a pathway to deeper hurts.

The good news is that they can be resolved, and often are resolved. In addition to relatives, there are others who are willing to sympathize and empathize with you. When you are hurt, there are others who go through pain as well. They are hurt, by your hurt.

Importance of Professionals

Hurting people exist among the billions of people living in the world. Many of them have life experiences such as starvation, hunger, disease, war, and homelessness. The vast majority will never have the opportunity to see trained medical professionals to aid in peace and healing.

We tend to go to the doctor for ailments to relieve pain. It is just as critical to seek professional help when one wants to end life.

Personal negative experiences of the *now* will often overshadow everything that was enjoyable in the past. They will also "cancel" future experiences to look back on for if suicide is the concluding decision.

Most of us love to look at pictures of the past that can then be shared with others in future relationships. These amusing memories of relationships and growth cannot be equaled. As I recall, it was positive memories and relationships that helped to bring about a change in my life. They can be just as rewarding for you too.

Memories

Think about one of the fun memories you have already had with one of your relatives. What did you laugh about? Where did you go? What did you do?

I will never forget the time when my family spent the day at my uncle Ted's house. He was the brother to my mother. Uncle Ted lived in the country where there were horses and cows and chickens. He also had a pond filled with fish and a river that you could fish in running through his property.

On one summer day Uncle Ted took me fishing with him in the river. Now most people I know fish with a rod-n-reel with a hook on the end of a line. Bait would be placed on the hook so that fish would be lured to the bait and get caught on the hook.

Not so for Uncle Ted. He fished with his bare hands, and sometimes with a pitchfork, and if he felt like it, he would use a rod-n-reel. On this day he was fishing with his bare hands.

I had never seen anyone fish with their bare hands. As I look back on that experience, I learned a different way of fishing. Up to that time, I thought there was only one-way to fish: baiting the hook, casting your line into the water, and waiting on the fish to bite method.

Life Lesson Two: Life Needs a Different Way to Fish

Life is often more complicated, than simply the bait on the hook, having the line in the water, and waiting on the fish to bite method. Sometimes what life needs is a different way of fishing. What does that mean?

It means that there are more answers to your situation than suicide and it should not be the only choice to be made in your mind and heart. In the chapter on *options* you will discover other ways to fish.

It was when I was just a *"baby"* that a relative taught me a valuable lesson about fishing and life.

"Suicide doesn't end the chances of life getting worse, it eliminates the possibility of ever getting better"

- UNKNOWN

Three

"I didn't because you were always there"

We Are Born to Cry

When a baby is born the sound of crying is one of the most heartwarming sounds you can hear. It is the baby's announcement to the parents, that I am here, and you will know it every day and every night with more of the same sounds.

People tend to feel better after a good cry. Crying produces tears that have healing properties. It is sort of like a good laugh. Somehow it relaxes the tensions and relieves the sadness.

Support for this idea can be found in an article titled *"Health Benefits of Tears"* written by Dr. Judith Orloff who states,

> For over twenty years as physician, I've witnessed, time and again, the healing power of tears. Tears are your body's release valve for stress, sadness, grief, anxiety, and frustration. Also, you can have tears of joy; say when a child is born or tears of relief when a difficulty has passed. In my own life, I am grateful when I can cry. It feels cleansing, a

way to purge pent up emotions so they don't lodge in my body as stress symptoms such as fatigue or pain. To stay healthy and release stress, I encourage my patients to cry. For both men and women, tears are a sign of courage, strength, and authenticity. (Orloff, 2011)

Powerful Men and Women Shed Tears

So from the very beginning of life tears may be good for healing. The article goes on to say,

> Crying makes us feel better, even when a problem persists. In addition to physical detoxification, emotional tears heal the heart. You don't want to hold tears back. Patients sometimes say, "Please excuse me for crying. I was trying hard not to. It makes me feel weak." My heart goes out to them when I hear this. I know where that sentiment comes from: parents who were uncomfortable around tears, a society that tells us we're weak for crying--in particular that "powerful men don't cry." I reject these notions. The new enlightened paradigm of what constitutes a powerful man and woman is someone who has the strength and self-awareness to cry. These are the people who impress me, not those who put up some macho front of faux-bravado. (Orloff, 2011)

In some arenas the behavioral expectation is that you cannot be seen as a person who sheds tears, especially if you are sports-minded, military-minded, or an initiation inductee in certain fraternities, where accepted behaviors in the organization must be complied with.

But without a doubt some of the most heart-warming scenes on television today are military men and women coming back home to unanticipated family members. Not only are family members in tears. In many cases hero's and heroines of military service are in tears. Furthermore, strangers like television anchor personalities are crying. Lastly we the viewers are crying.

Crying is a part of who we are. We cry the first day of birth. Although the actual tears may not form until later, the crying is already there. Tears are always a reliable source available to comfort us through difficult times.

A Time of Uncontrollable Tears

In 1998 I received a call that my father had died. At that time I was living in Florida and he was living in Tennessee. Because I loved my father I could not control the tears. For a while they were shed almost every day. It has been twenty years since that time, and in between those years there have been lots of other reasons to cry. It has not been for misery and tragedy only; I also had occasions to cry many tears of joy.

Orloff goes on to say,

> It is good to cry. It is healthy to cry. This helps to emotionally clear sadness and stress. Crying is also essential to resolve grief, when waves of tears periodically come over us after we experience a loss. Tears help us process the loss so we can keep living with open hearts. Otherwise, we are a set up for depression if we suppress these potent feelings. (Orloff, 2011)

Jonathan Rottenberg however somewhat disagrees with Orloff. He writes,

We recently analyzed over 3,000 detailed reports of recent crying episodes where respondents described the surrounding social context and the effects of crying on mood. We discovered that not all crying episodes are created equally. Criers who received social support during their crying episode were more likely to report mood benefits than criers who did not report receiving social support. Likewise, when the precipitating events of a crying episode had been resolved, mood benefits were more likely than when events were unresolved. Finally, criers who reported experiencing negative social emotions like shame and embarrassment were less likely to report mood benefits. (Rottenberg, 2010)

Even today, every now and then tears have been there for me. Babies are not the only ones crying. Teenagers cry. Young adults cry. Middle teenagers cry. And seniors cry. Tears are always there, and they are naturally summoned at the right time to comfort when one's chapters of life are difficult.

The Loyalty of Tears—The Big Edge

Jerry Jones the owner of the Dallas Cowboys was interviewed by Jenna Bush Hager the daughter of former President George W. Bush who asked Jones, "What was the most important lesson that you have learned from your family?" His response was "loyalty."

Then Jones told a wonderful story about a super bowl game involving Troy Aikman the then quarterback, and Jay Novacek the dependable tight end for the Cowboys. Jones said, "Aikman threw a football once to Novacek without even looking at him." Aikman was asked, "How could you have done that and not even look?

The response from Aikman was "I knew he was there. He is always there" Then Jones said, "That's a big edge". (*NBC Today*, 2016)

Tears are like that. Loyalty is a good way to describe tears. Tears will come to be with us no matter how difficult the pain may be. They will come to heal us at the moment when they are needed. When no one else is around, tears will always be there.

Life Lesson Three: *If You Are Able to Cry You Have a Big Edge*

David Brooks who writes for The New York Times says, "Emotions are not separate from reason, but they are the foundation of reason because they tell us what to value" (2011).

Did you know that all tears do not look the same; there are tears for different emotions, pain, and difficulties. But all of them are there to heal. That is a big edge.

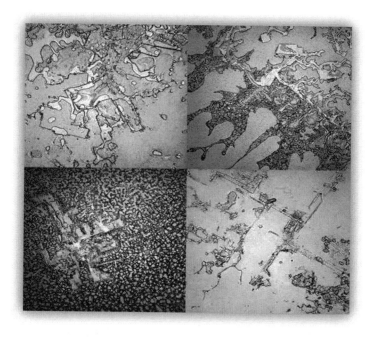

Provided are examples of four different tears photographed under a microscope: tears of laughter, hope, change, and grief. Rose-Lynn Fisher is the creator of these amazing pictures that show different tears all for our healing?

Elie Wiesel a Holocaust survivor and later human rights activist died at the age of 87. When Wiesel was 15, he was sent to Auschwitz concentration camp in Poland. He was later moved to the Buchenwald camp in Germany where he was liberated by the United States. Wiesel, speaking about tears, said, "When tragedy becomes too painful too deep you cannot speak; so the tears become words" (Remembering Elie Wiesel, July 8, 2016).

Very few people know what the longest verse in the Bible says, but the shortest verse in the Bible is one to be remembered. It simply says, "Jesus wept" (John 11:35)

"If you are looking for a sign not to kill yourself, this is it"

-UNKNOWN

Four

"I didn't because I didn't want to"

Why Do People Commit Suicide

Why do people commit suicide? There are many reasons. Hopelessness and pain rank among the top, but they are not the biggest reasons people commit suicide.

In an article titled "Why Do People Kill Themselves? New Warning Signs," the number one reason for suicide develops according to the author. "In general, people do not commit suicide because they are in pain, they commit suicide because they don't believe there is a reason to live and the world will be better off without them" (Kashdan, 2014).

What people really want is to have a little hope or perhaps have the pain to go away or to live in a world where they are significant and life is worth living. They don't really want to commit suicide.

The above article further states,

> "A person might also require the capacity to harm themselves. A person must be highly tolerant of pain and

conflict to make room for the uncomfortable thoughts and feelings that arise when working toward the goal of ending life. This tolerance of distress must be acquired somewhere along the way. Researchers continue to find support for the notion that the greatest suicidal risk exists for people that believe they are a burden on society AND possess a history where they acquired the capacity to harm themselves. This acquired capability can arise in unusual ways such as:

- playing violent and extreme sports
- getting multiple body piercings and tatoos
- shooting guns
- getting in physical fights

These types of painful and provocative events offer a sense of fearlessness about lethal self-injury." (Kashdan, 2014)

Veterans and Active Military Suicides

I was surprised to learn that about 22 veterans commit suicide every day. I was additionally surprised to learn that most soldiers who are active in the military who tried to commit suicide had not been deployed and most did so within the first six months.

Maggie Fox writes regarding military soldiers who commit suicide in her article "Military Suicides: Most Attempts Come Before Soldiers Ever See Combat."

> Most soldiers who attempt suicide haven't even been deployed yet, a new study finds. The period of highest

risk was just two months after starting military service, according to the study of more than 163,000 men and women in the Army. It found that 61 percent of those who tried to take their own lives had not yet been deployed. (Fox, 2016)

The following was written in a CNN Report: regarding some veterans,

> Whether it's physical and mental health challenges, financial woes, or what some describe as the "daunting task" of re-assimilating to civilian life, the pressure can be overwhelming. In fact, 22 veterans kill themselves every day, according to a report released in February of last year by the Department of Veterans Affairs. (Alarcon, 2015)

This means then that veteran suicides alone equal to over 8,000 a year. That is why this book is written. I want to help soldiers, active and veterans, as well as others find reasons to live.

The Heartbreaking Death of My Military Brother

My brother was an active duty military service in the late 1960s. He was a part of the 101st Airborne and died in Okinawa, Japan. While he was not a suicide fatality I will never forget the day when two military officers arrived at our door. Their faces told their message before they ever spoke one word.

A one-word description of how the family felt on that day would be "*devastation.*" *Heartbroken* would be another one word description. He was the oldest brother and I was the youngest of four boys along with three sisters in the family.

I must say it has taken over forty years to get over his death; although, I am not sure I ever have. Then multiply my grief by eight, for that was the number of immediate family members who were immersed in grief by the loss of his life.

Life Lesson Four: A Heartbroken Family Is a Hurting Family

I know what it is like to be a part of a military family that receives the horrifying news that a loved one has died. The memory of the heartbreak felt by my family over my brother's death was a part of the thoughts that prevented me from committing suicide. I didn't want to bring the devastation and heartbrokenness to my family once again. I just didn't want to.

When you get into a tight place and everything goes against you, till it seems as though you could not hang on a minute longer, never give up then, for that is just the place and time that the tide will turn"

— HARRIET BEECHER STOWE

Five

"I DIDN'T BECAUSE THERE WERE OTHER OPTIONS"

To be Here or Not to be Here
"To be or not to be" is the question.

> "To be, or not to be . . ." is the opening phrase of a soliloquy in the "Nunnery Scene"[1] of William Shakespeare's play *Hamlet*. In the speech, a despondent Prince Hamlet contemplates death and suicide while waiting for Ophelia, the love of his life. He bemoans the pains and unfairness of life but acknowledges the alternative might be still worse." (*To be, or not to be*. Shakespeare, Wikipedia.org)

Hamlet hesitates in the play to make the final choice to commit suicide. He weighs his options and considers that suicide could be the worse option. Besides what would an after-life mean for him if he did consider suicide?

Here, Hamlet considers at length taking his own life. While he's feeling melancholy, we might even say depressed, over the death of his father, he's still hesitant to go so far as to kill himself. He worries about the repercussions. Specifically, he's worried about going to hell: "For in that sleep of death what dreams may come." Hamlet's reflection on death is significant because it highlights the intellectual importance of death and the afterlife in the play. Shakespeare is presenting a multifaceted exploration of death by having Hamlet analyze all the potential scenarios that could play out if he did commit suicide. (Study.com, Death in Hamlet)

Living Long Is a Great Life Option
So let's analyze other options that have real life potential rather than suicide. Earlier in Chapter Two I mentioned a woman who was approaching 108 years old whom I had the privilege of taking a picture with. The year of the picture taken was 2015. This would mean that she was born around 1907.

Take some time to think of all the life experiences she had. Now it would be naive to think that she did not have any bad experiences. I am sure she did. But she also had some great experiences. The conveniences we have today were not available in her early in life. I think it is safe to say life was very difficult.

Just four years before she was born, on December 17, 1903 the Wright brothers flew the first airplane called the Kitty Hawk. This means she probably did not fly in an airplane in her early years.

When she was born the Model T Ford car was not yet invented. The car came off the assembly line in 1908. The main way of transportation was walking or riding a horse. Imagine having to walk almost everywhere you wanted to go. There weren't many options to choose from for medical help, professional work, or even organized volunteer work. I'd like to offer some life options to be considered if you or someone you know needs help.

Life Lesson Five: There Is Only One of You But a World of Options

Options

OPTION 1: SEEK MEDICAL/PROFESSIONAL HELP

Seek professional help. There could be a medical situation like severe depression that needs to be explored. The mind and emotions need healing like the rest of the body. When it is clear that there are no underlying medical issues consider the following options to lower the stress of day-to-day issues that weigh you down.

OPTION 2: TALK TO A FRIEND OR RELATIVE

If you are thinking about harming yourself and you are the only person that knows, then you are only listening to yourself. And you are certainly not the best person to consult for counsel, given the fact that you have self-destructive intentions. A friend or relative who will lead you away from suicide to medical professional help or at least a supportive listening ear is better than being alone when the cry for help comes.

OPTION 3: SUPPORT GROUPS

Join a support group. You will discover there are people among the thousands who are depressed from a lesser to a greater degree. There are small groups you can join who understand your predicament and whose facilitator will walk you through the support you need.

OPTION 4: SEEK A NEW ENVIRONMENT

What may be needed is a new environment, a new start. Where you are living now might not be so healthy for you. This option should not be used purely for escape however, for there may be issues that need to be resolved and you will simply continue those issues in the new environment. A new environment may stimulate new and better reflections. In addition, going on a vacation could be the separation needed to clear your mind.

OPTION 5: SERVICE TO OTHERS

1. Volunteer to take care of an elderly person. You can start with those in your own family.
2. Talk to them about life experiences. The elderly are lonely and it is amazing what can be learned from those who have lived life.
3. Cut the grass of those who are elderly.
4. Clean their home.
5. Do errands for them.
6. Volunteer or work in a homeless shelter.
7. Help someone with his or her groceries.

OPTION 6: DO SOMETHING FUN

1. White Water Rafting
2. Hiking
3. Putt Putt Golfing
4. Go Cart Racing
5. Painting
6. Bowling
7. Amusement Parks

Why I Didn't and Why You Shouldn't Commit Suicide

OPTION 7: CHANGE DEFEAT INTO ACCOMPLISHMENT

At age 5 his Father died.
At age 16 he quit school.
At age 17 he had already lost four jobs.
At age 18 he got married.
Between ages 18 and 22, he was a railroad conductor and failed.
He joined the army and washed out there.
He applied for law school but was rejected.
He became an insurance salesman and failed again.
At age 19 he became a father.
At age 20 his wife left him and took their baby daughter.
He became a cook and dishwasher in a small cafe.
He failed in an attempt to kidnap his own daughter, and eventually he convinced his wife to return home.
At age 65 he retired.
On the 1st day of retirement he received a check from the Government for $105.
He felt that the Government was saying that he couldn't provide for himself.
He decided to commit suicide, it wasn't worth living anymore; he had failed so much.
He sat under a tree writing his will, but instead, he wrote what he would have accomplished with his life. He realized there was much more that he hadn't done. There was one thing he could do better than anyone he knew. And that was how to cook. So he borrowed $87 against his check and bought and fried up some chicken

using his recipe, and went door to ``door to sell them to his neighbors in Kentucky.

Remember at age 65 he was ready to commit suicide.

But at age 88 Colonel Sanders, founder of the Kentucky Fried Chicken (KFC) Empire was a billionaire.

Moral of the story: Attitude. It's never too late to start all over. MOST IMPORTANLY, IT'S ALL ABOUT YOUR ATTITUDE. NEVER GIVE UP NO MATTER HOW HARD IT GETS.

You have what it takes to be successful. Go for it and make a difference. No guts no glory. It's never too old to dream.

(The Inspiring Stuff Colonel Sanders, www.facebook.com)

"*If you want to show me that you really love me, don't say that you would die for me, instead stay alive for me.*"

- UNKNOWN

Six

"I didn't because other's didn't"

"He Who Wants to be Great Let Him Serve"

Many people have either tried to commit suicide or thought about it. The accomplishments of those who didn't are amazing.

As we saw with Colonel Sander's, things may not get better immediately but because you have passed the contemplation chapter in your life or even the attempt to commit suicide. You are now ready for the next adventure, that of being useful in life for yourself, and others.

In this chapter we will see how others, like Colonel Sanders, made an impact in life in different ways, because they didn't really want to commit suicide. Perhaps, you won't either, because you are already one of the great ones.

William Cowper Composer

I would like to start off with the name of William Cowper, poet and composer. Born November 15, 1731, Cowper was physically frail and later known to be very sensitive. Chances are you have never heard of his name, but you have heard of his music.

> In spite of his intellectual achievements, William Cowper was physically frail and emotionally sensitive throughout his childhood. One of the traumatic experiences that contributed to his emotional instability was the death of his mother when he was only six years old. Unable to properly deal with this grief that he experienced as a small child, it stayed with him throughout his life. He never stopped grieving for his mother. Even though he passed his law examination and was licensed as a lawyer, the very prospect of appearing before the bar for his final examination frightened him to the extent that he had a mental breakdown from which he never recovered. (*There Is a Fountain,* 2005)

Unfortunately Cowper tried to commit suicide several times. Cowper wrote many songs but one of the most beloved is *"There Is a Fountain Filled with Blood."*

Despite his emotional condition this song has restored many individuals to wholeness. Though he himself was in pain, he did a lot for those who were also in pain.

"Cowper also wrote a poem called 'The Negro's Complaint' (1788) which rapidly became very famous, and was often quoted by Dr. Martin Luther King Jr. during the 20th century civil rights movement." Some of the words to "The Negro's Complaint" are:

Why I Didn't and Why You Shouldn't Commit Suicide

> Men from England bought and sold me,
>   Paid my price in paltry gold;
> But, though slave they have enrolled me,
>   Minds are never to be sold.
> Prove that you have human feelings,
>   Ere you proudly question ours!
> (William Cowper, wikipedia.org)

Celebrities

- In 2016, MMA fighter Ronda Rousey revealed that she contemplated suicide after her devastating 2015 loss to Holly Holm. Although she didn't actually take physical steps to hurt herself, Rousey said that she seriously thought about it because her undefeated streak was over . . . the love of her family, friends, and boyfriend, Travis Browne, ultimately persuaded her otherwise.
- Drew Barrymore attempted suicide by cutting her wrists with a kitchen knife when she was just 14 years old.
- Elton John tried to kill himself by sticking his head in a glass stove and breathing in the deadly gases. He wrote the song "Someone Saved My Life Tonight" about the event.
- Halle Berry told *People Magazine* that she attempted to commit suicide after her marriage to David Justice ended. She said, "I was sitting in my car, and I knew the gas was coming when I had an image of my mother finding me."

- Princess Diana tried to commit suicide by throwing herself down a flight of stairs because she was so distraught over how Prince Charles treated her.
- Johnny Cash tried to commit suicide in 1969, while he was high on drugs, by getting lost in the Nickajack Cave.
- Tina Turner revealed that she tried to kill herself in 1986 in her autobiography.
- Richard Pryor tried to commit suicide by pouring rum on his body and lighting himself on fire in 1980.
- Mike Tyson blames promoter Don King for manipulating and using him, which led to his depression, drug use, and suicide attempt.
- Walt Disney attempted to overdose on drugs and alcohol when he was 31 years old. (Celebrities ranker, 2016)

There are many more celebrities that could be added to this list; however, suicide is not to be glamorized. It crosses all socio-economic barriers.

Life Lesson Six: Have a person and a cause that gives you a reason to live.

I Wanted to Live so I Didn't

There are many others who the world will never know who wanted to commit suicide. It can happen to anyone at any age, but it doesn't have to. And in most cases those who attempt suicide really don't want to. You don't have to be a celebrity to be frustrated with life. I like others have had my frustrations but I still wanted to live.

Why I Didn't and Why You Shouldn't Commit Suicide

I wanted to live and be "somebody" one day. I wanted to travel and see the rest of the world. I wanted my life to change. I didn't really want to take my life. Finally I got the change I was looking for. So *I didn't*.

"Place your hand over your heart, can you feel it? That is called purpose. You're alive for a reason so don't ever give up"

- UNKNOWN

Seven

"I didn't because my pockets were empty"

Empty Pockets

Growing up in cities can be challenging even when trying to do simple things like walking to school as a daily routine. I remember hearing a story of a young man who was robbed as he went to school of his lunch money. Every time the thieves stopped him, he was asked to empty his pockets. It happened so frequently in that neighborhood that it became expected.

Oh but the young man came up with a brilliant idea. Instead of waiting to be asked by the opportunist thieves to empty his pockets, he would simply pull the inside of all his pockets out. Now upon approaching the thieves on his daily walk to school they would let him pass by after seeing his pockets were empty.

Envy The Jealousy of Others

What if your neighbor drove up in a brand new car. And your car is a jacked-up jalopy that smoked. There may be a touch of envy. But what if you discovered later that the brand new car was really for you. Your neighbor bought it for you. Now you are the one driving the brand new car. What feelings do you suppose you would have as you see others with jacked-up jalopies that smoke?

I have had a few jacked-up jalopies in my life. I can tell you having navigated through the potholes of life in them were some of the great stories of living life with empty pockets. When you make it through you are better and stronger having gone through seasons of empty pockets.

Life should mean more than what you have or don't have in your pockets. Actually, whether your pockets are in or out should not be the determining factor of whether one should commit suicide or not. At birth we all are born with empty pockets. When our lives are over our pockets will be just as empty as they were at our birth.

People Are More Important Than Things
The people, who were your predecessors, siblings, and friends just to name a few, are more important than your pockets. Besides, your children care little about whether your pockets are lined with silver and gold. They care more about a relationship with mom and dad. They care about a day at the park. They care about hikes in nature. They care about tucking them in for bed and bedtime stories. They care about hugs and kisses when they are in pain. They don't care about empty pockets. There are some things money cannot buy.

So in case you have forgotten some of the wonderful quotes about money, this is a good place to reiterate what money can and cannot buy.

Why I Didn't and Why You Shouldn't Commit Suicide

> A bed but not sleep
> Computer but not a brain
> Food but not an appetite
> Finery but not beauty
> A house but not a home
> Medicine but not health
> Luxuries but not culture
> Amusements but not happiness
> Acquaintance but not friends
> Obedience but not faithfulness
> Sex but not love

(AUTHOR UNKNOWN)

One of the best quotes I have seen lately about money is:

> *"It's good to have money and the things that money can buy, but it is good, too, to check up once and a while and make sure that you haven't lost the things that money can't buy"*

(LORIMER, G.,) (N. D.)

Things like sleep, a brain, an appetite, a beating heart, home, health, happiness, friends, faithfulness and love are far more important than money.

However, as one grows from empty pockets at birth to maturity, personal interest develops and money is necessary for essentials as daily food, housing and transportation. These necessities are only to aid you; they are not to define you.

When we see someone drive a luxury car or live in a luxurious home that we cannot afford, there is a tendency to think others are better in ways that we are not. When frustration arises because we cannot meet our financial obligations, then suicide for some seems to be an option.

So how does that improve the empty pockets issue? For it is dangerous to fall into the mistaken trap that others will be better off financially if you were not here.

Comparable Comparison
So let's think about this again. You came here with empty pockets and when life is over you leave with empty pockets. But now because you are going through an empty pocket season, suicide is an option? I understand it is painful and help is not coming fast enough.

I don't want to belittle what you are going through in your season of empty pockets or compare your pockets with others, but lets for a moment do just that; lets compare your situation with others who are worse off than you. I have heard of people living in situations so bad that garbage landfills become their last hope. Some have no hospitals to go to. No legs. No doctors to treat them. No food to eat. Some do not only have empty pockets they don't have pockets.

My Experience of Empty Pockets
As a young boy I grew up in a house with a sign that said, "Unfit for Human Habitation". Although it might have affected my parents I never noticed it was a problem to them. It was not a problem to me either when I was growing up; but the sign placed later on the house was a hint of poverty.

In addition to this there was a time when my wife and I along with our four children had become homeless for a short while. We were not living under the interstate but we were in our car traveling from one state to another, then back to where home use to be.

Finally, pride gave way to my predicament and I called someone I had known for only about a year. I told him my situation and he invited my family and me over to stay at his house. I had pockets but they were empty. We slept on their living room floor until we could find a place to live two weeks later. Honestly it felt like two years later.

We were finally able to find a place to live. We were finally able to sleep in our own beds. We were able to buy groceries and place food in our own refrigerator. We were finally able to enjoy our own back yard and feel a sense of gratefulness that our lives had turned around.

Life Lesson Seven: Use the season of empty pockets to learn and grow.

Empty Pockets Are Usually Periodic

Whenever we live life with empty pockets it seems those conditions will never change. The fact is, things can turn around quickly or gradually but it usually turns around. It may be simply a matter of getting the right job or just getting a job. Sometimes it is a matter of money management. Sometimes it is a matter of changing some old habits with money. Sometimes there are physical illnesses that need to heal that would enable empty pockets to continue for a long time.

The question is often asked, when will the empty pockets end. There is no set time frame for empty pockets. All I know is that it is usually temporary. But however long it takes; it is good not to see the experience as insignificant. Use the season to learn and grow for our value is more than what we have in our pockets. We are valuable because significance has been bestowed upon us from the beginning.

The Value Is Not In Your Pockets

You can go beyond your dreams. One of the best ways to see your value is to invest in others. The best thing that you can do is live for others. It is great to give to others from pockets that are full. But giving from the position of empty pockets is marvelous. Plan to be a blessing to others everyday, and as you do, your own pockets will be running over. From the gratefulness of your heart let your gratitude flow.

Philip a Boy Born With Downs Syndrome

Perhaps you have heard about Phillip. Philip was a boy born with Downs Syndrome. Philip along with nine other children in the third grade went to school everyday.

Youngsters as well as adults sometimes will pick on others who seem to be different from them. If need be, let others know about any mistreatment that you may be experiencing. It is important that there is accountability for misbehaving.

"Philip was not really a part of the group. Philip did not choose, nor did he want to be different. He just was. And that was the way things were." (Harvey, 1993)

However the teacher saw opportunities to teach the children about love, kindness and character.

The teacher had a great idea to collect and put to use the plastic egg-shaped pantyhose containers. All the children were to go outside and find something with the "symbol of life" and place it in the plastic egg-shaped containers and returning to reveal life in each egg.

"They would then open and share their new life symbols and surprises, one by one.

It was glorious. It was confusing. It was wild. They ran all around the church grounds, gathering their symbols, and returned to the classroom.

They put all the eggs on a table, and then the teacher began to open them. All the children gathered around the table. He opened one and there was a flower, and they ooh-ed and aah-ed. He opened another and there was a little butterfly. "Beautiful!" the girls all said, since it is hard for eight-year old boys to say 'beautiful.' He opened another and there was a rock. And as third-graders will, some laughed, and some said, "That's crazy! How's a rock supposed to be like new life?" But the smart little boy who'd put it in there spoke up: "That's mine. And I knew all of you would get flowers and buds and leaves and butterflies and stuff like that. So I got a rock because I wanted to be different. And for me, that's new life." They all laughed.

The teacher said something about the wisdom of eight-year olds and opened the next one. There was nothing inside. The children, as eight-year olds will, said, "That's not fair. That's stupid! Somebody didn't do it right."

Then the teacher felt a tug on his shirt, and he looked down. "It's mine, Philip said. It's mine."

And the children said, "You don't ever do things right, Philip. There's nothing there!"

"I did so do it right!" Philip said. "I did do it right. The tomb is empty!"

There was silence, a very full silence. And for people who don't believe in miracles, I want to tell you that one happened that day. From that time on, it was different. Philip suddenly became a part of that group of eight-year old children. They took him in. He was set free from the tomb of his differentness.

Philip died last summer. His family had known since the time he was born that he wouldn't live out a full life span. Many other things were wrong with his little body. And so, late last July, with an infection that most normal children could have quickly shrugged off, Philip died.

At his memorial service, nine eight-year old children marched up to the altar, not with flowers to cover over the stark reality of death . . . but nine eight-year olds, along with their . . . teacher, marched right up to that altar, and laid on it an empty egg . . . an empty, old, discarded pantyhose egg." (Harry H. Pritchett Jr. originator, Retold by Harvey, 1993)

What I like about the story of Philip is that his empty pockets ended when he was alive not at death. Philip was included and his differentness was set free. His situation was temporary. Financial problems like homelessness are temporary. Tombs are temporary. We have been set free at someone else's expense. Therefore, we should set others free by the motivation of gratefulness. By doing this you will become unaware that you have pockets.

*"Suicide is a permanent solution
to a temporary problem"*

Eight

"I didn't because I was only down, not defeated"

Defeat Defeatism

A former bouncer in a marathon dance hall, Horace McCoy, titled his first novel, published in 1935, "They Shoot Horses, Don't They?" Its theme was defeatism in life's long dance, its style hard-boiled; its plot centered on the killing of a marathon dancer, a hopeless derelict, by her partner, out of what the murderer insisted was kindness, as "the only way to put her out of her misery." (Safire, 1997)

Never in real life should one act as the judge and jury for someone else's pain by taking their life. While one's own personal pain needs to be acknowledged, the killing of others to prevent them also from hurting is unsound.

This murder, suicide as depicted in the novel/movie is the example of sick and self-regarding persons who takes upon themselves the tragic taking of the lives of others. It is known as "supremacy crimes," when individuals want control over their lives and others.

What gets lost in this fictitious character of the derelict woman was that she was down but not defeated. She was determined to keep going despite what others said or thought about her, and despite what she thought about herself.

Mistakes Are a Part of Being Human

Blunders from the past, mistakes in the present, or grief of the future will have their influence. They can cause us to sorrow. But these blunders, mistakes, and grief's are the result of being human.

Ronald Reagan, who served as the 40th president of the United States, was known to say, "You know, by the time you've reached my age, you've made plenty of mistakes if you've lived your life properly" (Pinkney, 2003).

Depression is a condition that everyone experiences at some point or another. For sure, depression can interrupt the normalcy of our lives but it does not need to ruin life.

As we have seen in the previous chapter, the rich, the poor, the well known, and not-so-well known get depressed. Depressive situations will arise that are unpredictable and unpreventable to you and by you.

Okay, let's take a test. Check the block that applies to you.

1. Have you ever lied before? ( )
2. Have you ever lied about lying? ( )

3. Have you ever had thoughts or feelings you thought inappropriate? ( )
4. Have you ever washed your colored clothes with white clothes in hot water using bleach? ( )
5. Have you ever locked your car keys in the car? ( )
6. Have you ever accused someone or been accused of something that neither they nor you did? ( )
7. Have you ever stolen something that did not belong to you? ( )

Whatever your answers: things, people, and life mean something to you. Honesty means something to you. Your car keys means something to you. Having a reasonably clear mind mean something to you. (I say reasonably because the mind is like dreams, you cannot always keep your mind from bad thoughts no more can you decide on all your dreams). But what you discover is that you care. You care about others as well as your own feelings.

When the weight of these mistakes, failures, and grief moves from just an interference or interruption, to extinction of ones life, then for those who survive the loss of a loved one the grief continues because they care.

Adverse occurrences can happen in normal natural settings and all are not considered to be wrong or right. Other occasions are more serious and demand a change in behavior; however, none need lead to suicide for every person is of great value.

A Fatal False Teaching
Contrary to the philosophical teachings of fatalism, all lives are sacred and significant, and one should not give in to its idea.

Friedrich Nietzsche lived in the eighteenth century and became famous for the maxim "God is dead." Whether you believe in God or not is not my issue for now, but how Nietzsche's philosophical teachings influenced the idea of suicide becomes the primary focus.

Living life according to Nietzsche is meaningless or nothingness. Nietzsche basically found no value in life because as he saw it life is an endless circle. It has no real beginning and no real end. It is an exercise in futility. Giving in to that kind of existence leaves no future to gain, only a life of empty meaning.

You can begin to see how this approach to life becomes detrimental. If all you are, and all you do are meaningless, then why live? It all comes to nothing.

The Problem of Life Without Meaning

The problem with Nietzsche's message is that it sends a hopeless, trapped, despairing, communication to one already down. There is nothing to hope for; nothing to believe in, and when it comes to feelings they often betray us of the real reality of how things are.

Again, as was said earlier, all of us are depressed at some time. But countless people have gone beyond their depression to live productive lives. They are the down but not defeated ones.

How then can life be down but not defeated? How can life be lived beyond depression to productive living? If it is to be done at all, it must happen when one sees purpose. In addition, they must see themselves as not only for themselves but living to help others as well.

Life Lesson Eight: You Cannot Control What Others Do to You But You Can Control What You Do for Others

As I end this chapter I would like to leave you with some quotes to help you towards the victory you seek from courageous fallen personalities taken from (www.brainyquote.com 2016, key word "defeated").

"Only a man who knows what it is like to be defeated can reach down to the bottom of his soul and come up with the extra ounce of power it takes to win when the match is even." (Muhammad Ali)

"Defeat doesn't finish a man, quit does. A man is not finished when he's defeated. He's finished when he quits." (Richard M. Nixon)

"Being defeated is often a temporary condition. Giving up is what makes it permanent." (Marilyn vos Savant)

"The past cannot be changed. The future is yet in your power"

- UNKNOWN

Nine

"I DIDN'T BECAUSE I KNEW SOMEBODY LOVED ME"

Too Young to Love

At the age of six I had a crush on another six-year-old girl. Later I had a crush on Doris Day a Hollywood movie star, but she did not even know I existed. It is sort of like young people putting up poster pictures in their dorm room of some known personalities who have hundreds of admirers.

However, when I was in my early teens I believed I was in love. But there came a time when the one I thought I loved told me that it was over. Over. Yes, over. I thought I was going to die. The pain was unpleasant to say the least.

You see, I was told of our breakup in the wintertime. There was nothing left for me to do but to walk home in the snow, which was about five to six inches deep. The temperature had to be freezing or close to freezing.

As I was walking home I can remember tears running down my face. At the time, I thought I would never get over it. Furthermore, I felt it necessary to protect myself in the future from that awful feeling by saying I would never love again.

Love Worth Finding

One of the best lines in literature is "and it came to pass" or "in the process of time" or "by and by." These lines are used to reveal a transition of what happened in the past, to a brand new life situation.

The new life situation was when I met my wife in my early twenties while attending school. She was and still is beautiful. I was starting to thaw from my freeze to love again.

"And it came to pass" that we dated and eventually got married. "In the process of time" we now have four children. "By and by" I will even sing a love song to her.

I recall a time when I was going through a personal crisis as fellow workers and I were riding a bus to attend a meeting. As I looked out the window I started thinking about my wife and how much she meant to me. So I got out my pen and paper to write a poem out of my heart's true feelings for her.

What am I trying to say? I am trying to say that if you have a broken heart and you feel you cannot go on in life, "in the process of time" healing of your brokenness is not only possible but also likely. You can love again.

Unfortunately, I cannot tell you when the hurt will feel better and it is important that you don't just throw yourself to any relationship that comes your way. If that happens, it can set you up for more hurt.

Lost Love and Suicide

When the heart is hurt by love, it is a vulnerable time for thoughts of suicide. It feels like the pain and the hurt just won't go away.

Sometimes individuals think themselves to be undesirable or less desirable. Sometimes it is difficult to adjust to the social environment and the questions one might be asked by others.

Why I Didn't and Why You Shouldn't Commit Suicide

There is another way of looking at it. What if there is someone else for you, and you just don't know it? What if your value is more than a disappointing relationship and you just don't know it? What if your future is waiting for your potential and success? What if hope is longing to be gratified with fulfillment and you just don't know it?

What if the pain in your heart keeps you just outside the reality that others really care about you and they are willing to reveal a capacity to love, and you just don't know it?

What He Didn't Know

> Several years ago a rag-covered creature was captured in the jungles of Guam. Underneath the tattered clothing, long hair, and skin scars was a Japanese soldier. Astonishment swept the island at the thought of a man hiding for twenty-five years after the war ended. (Spangler, 1977, p. 165)
>
> For most of the 28 years that Shoichi Yokoi, a lance corporal in the Japanese Army of World War II, was hiding in the jungles of Guam, he firmly believed his former comrades would one day return for him. (Lanchin, 2013)

In the same article Yokoi's own memoirs were used to tell his amazing story. His memoirs were published in Japanese two years after his discovery, as well as the testimony of those who found him that day. Hatashin spent years piecing together his uncle's dramatic story. His book, *Private Yokoi's War and Life on Guam, 1944-1972,* was published in English in 2009. "Yokoi's own memoirs of his time in hiding reveal his desperation not to give up hope, especially in the last eight years when he was totally alone—his last two surviving companions died in floods in 1964" (Lanchin 2012).

The sad fact about Shoichi Yokoi according to Spangler was that for over twenty years the war had been over and he *just didn't know.*

Photos taken from *BBC News*, January 24, 2012.

Life Lesson Nine: *In the Process of Time Love Will Blossom Again. Do Not Close the Heart When You Are Hurt in a Love Relationship.*

I close this chapter with a famous quote. For so many years I thought Robert Kennedy was the author of it. Kennedy certainly made it famous though. But this quote is from George Bernard Shaw and can be found in *The Complete Pocket Positives* by Pinkney (2003). It is not just a quote; it is an aspiration to pursue your purpose.

"Some men see things as they are and say 'Why?' I dream things that never were and say 'Why not?'" George Bernard Shaw

"Sometimes God doesn't change your situation because He's trying to change your heart"

Ten

"I didn't because there were
many uncertainties"

What Happens When a Person Dies

The age-old question of what happens when one dies is asked in every generation. It will continue to be a mystery to some even though some things appear to be clear. For instance, it is clear life is ended. Life as one knows it ceases when one dies.

Even with this understanding about death, there is another question, not about death, but about living. The question is, if I die shall we live again?.

Where Does One Go When They Die

Another uncertainty for some is, where does one go when they die? Do they go to heaven, hell, or some place called purgatory? Do they go through transmigration or do they go to the grave? If they go to the grave, will they have an opportunity to live again, and where and under what set of conditions will one live again? It will take a lot more time and lot more space to answer all these questions.

However in most religious beliefs there is some understanding that life will continue, in some way, or in some form even after death. The paramount questions that come to mind are, when? And is it for my good or for my evil?

When it comes to suicide a certain question almost always emerges; "Will a person who commits suicide be saved, or are they lost?" I will answer *this* question definitively at the end of this chapter but before I do I would like to tell you a true story about a person who committed suicide.

A Personal Experience of a Suicide

I was working with a local police department as a resource person between the community and the police department when I received a call to an active shooting incident. I immediately jumped in the unmarked police car that was provided to me when I was on call.

When I arrived at the scene the streets were blocked off to prevent others from carelessly walking in the line of gunfire. I immediately reported to the officer in charge and was instructed to go to the family members who were already near the shooting location.

In my inquiry of the family members about the shooter, I soon discovered I knew the man who had fired the shots. I had visited the home several times.

I later discovered that he had shot his wife, though not fatally. She was able to flee from her husband and away from the house, and was already on enroute to the hospital by ambulance.

Why I Didn't and Why You Shouldn't Commit Suicide

The husband was still in the house but no one knew what the situation was like inside the house. After hours of standoff it was decided to send a robot in and then later to send in the "swat team" to end the standoff.

Cameras were attached to the robot that communicated and confirmed the husband was lying on the floor. From the pictures the swat team concluded that he had committed suicide.

Someone needed to inform the wife that her husband was no longer living and had ended his life at his own hands. I made the decision to volunteer to be the one to do it because I was on duty and I knew the family. Needless to say this was a very emotionally, exhausting day.

Words of Comfort to the Family

As the family made preparations for the funeral service I was asked by the family to give words of comfort at the funeral to the family members. I consented to do whatever I could.

There had been some discussion already within the family as to whether or not this father, grandfather, brother, and uncle would be saved after taking his own life, so I sought to tackle the question that was already on the minds of the family.

The reason this question comes up in the first place is because in the Bible in Deuteronomy 5:17 says, "Thou shalt not kill" (murder). Therefore one would say if you killed yourself it is included in the violation.

Example of Samson

I had heard a minister speak about a biblical character by the name of Samson who had committed suicide. The reference to

Samson was not found in the Old Testament but in the New Testament. Only three words were used, "and of Samson." These words in the book of Hebrews are found in chapter eleven, verse thirty-two. Three words easily overlooked.

What is interesting is that the whole chapter of Hebrews eleven mentions the faithful people of the Bible. The chapter is often referred to as "The Hall of Faith." And somewhere in the middle of the chapter Samson is mentioned as being one of the faithful.

Samson died asking God for strength one more time or for the last time. He would push two pillars down on his enemies and himself, therefore dying in the process. Yet he is mentioned in "The Hall of Faith" with others like Abraham and Moses.

In the case of this man who shot his wife and then himself, it was an unfortunate occurrence. The pain and hurt were evident the day of the funeral. The family was also divided on his final destiny with many questions. Would he be lost? Would he be saved? Did he have a chance to repent?

One other detail is important to know, and that is before his suicide he had been ill. It is uncertain as to how much his illness played a part in his decision.

I thought it would be a real tragedy to leave the family for the rest of their lives with some sort of knowledge that this man was lost. Instead I left them with these three words, " . . . and of Samson, . . ."

Life Lesson Ten: *It would be presumptuous to think if one commits suicide that they will be like Samson in "The Hall of Faith"*

A Definitive Answer on Suicide

The definitive answer to the question of this man being saved or lost is, *I don't know, we don't know.* We can be quick to put people in heaven or hell. The real definitive truth is, *we don't know*. This is not to deny a heaven or a hell.

To be clear suicide is tragic. It brings misery. There are reasons one should not do it. It would be presumptuous to think that one is saved as Samson. At the same time we must recognize that Samson is in "The Hall of Faith.

These matters will ultimately not be decided by any of us. Therefore, if we don't know and the choices are will I live the rest of my life with despair or hope; as the pastor concluded we should not live a burdened-down life, why not live in hope. Allow God to answer the ultimate question.

"I know the plans I have for you . . . to prosper you and not to harm you, plans to give you hope and a future"

Eleven

"I didn't because troubles have benefits"

We Are Strengthened

You cannot get away from trials and troubles. When we go *through* trials and troubles there may be a purpose behind it. And I really do mean *go through*.

As painful as they are, the one going through trials and troubles becomes strengthened as he/she endures them. We are made to go through adversity but going through them with a sense of purpose is essential to human growth.

We Have Purpose

I love animals, for animals bring incredible admiration. Though I don't have any animals at this time, I've had fish, worms, a cat, about six dogs, three birds, butterflies, and on occasion ants, spiders, crabs and a turtle.

Some of these animals, especially dogs, are raised with a purpose. In fact in some circles they are called "dogs with a purpose."

When they are raised with a purpose they must go through training (trials) to be the greatest support for their owner. The owner's may suffer from some type of aliment and the purpose of the dog is to make life better for the owner.

People who go through trials are some of the strongest people on earth. Instead of being weak and pathetic, they tend to understand, sympathize, and empathize with others who are going through similar problems; for they have endured the grit and grim of life.

The Depth of Power on the Inside

Nelson Mandela spent twenty-seven years in prison in South Africa for basically being against Apartheid (a segregated political system) yet he became the first black president of South Africa.

Many thought he would take revenge on the people who treated him badly. Instead, what made him such a great man was the fact that he was willing to forgive.

Bill Clinton, the former U.S. President, told the United Nations in July 2013 that he had praised Mandela on his decision to invite his jailer to his inauguration and to include white opposition parties into his government.

> Mr. Clinton asked Mandela: "Tell me the truth: when you were walking down the road that last time didn't you hate them?" Mandela answered: "I did. I am old enough to tell the truth . . . I felt hatred and fear but I said to myself, if you hate them when you get in that car you will still be their prisoner. I wanted to be free and so I let it go." (Malala, 2016)

Anything at all that looks like revenge makes you a prisoner. Sometimes the revenge is motivated by how you feel at the moment. But you are made for another purpose, not to be a prisoner to revengeful feelings and thoughts. Mandela once said, "It is in your hands to make of our world a better place."

What Are You Running From

Someone has said, "Suicide is the easy way out." I am not so sure that it is easy, but it would be more rewarding if time were spent making the world a better place. Somebody needs the purpose you were made for.

Perhaps you are unaware that there was a prophet of God according to the Bible who became suicidal. His name was Jonah. He was suicidal because he was running from God's command to warn the people of Nineveh to turn from their wicked ways.

So he boarded a boat going in the opposite direction of where God wanted him to go and the sea became furious. The reason the sea became furious as far as Jonah was concerned, was because he did not want to do what the Lord told him to do. Therefore, he became suicidal instead of being a man of purpose.

Self: The Wrong Place to Care

Jonah was a man who cared not for others, but for himself. He did not even reveal his designed plan of running away until the casting of lots (an ancient way of identifying a troublemaker). And when the lot fell on him he suggested that they cast him overboard into the sea.

Jonah was ready to put a period on his life while God's purpose was to put a comma. Therefore, according to the Bible in the book of Jonah it says, "Now the Lord prepared a great fish to swallow up Jonah. And Jonah was in the belly of the fish three days and three nights" (Jonah 1:17).

Jonah did not die; instead he ended up praying to God about his affliction and "the Lord spake unto the fish, and it vomited out Jonah on dry land" (Jonah 2:10).

When you go through trials and troubles and especially those not of your choosing, those trials and troubles can have benefits. The benefits may be to face future troubles or to accomplish some future purpose. The trials are preparation for accomplishment.

Although Jonah was reluctant at first and had issues with being the person for the purpose of God, albeit, being in the belly of a fish became a great motivation for the purpose to be accomplished.

The city turned from their ways and sought the Lord. "And God saw their works, that they turned from their evil way; and God repented of the evil, that he had said that he would do unto them; and he did it not" (Jonah 3:10).

One of greatest quotes I have ever seen is the one found below. It is so great I framed the words on my wall.

Life Lesson Eleven:
What He says He
Will do in judgment . . .
If we turn from evil,
He will end up not doing
On account of His Mercy
Jeremiah 18:7-8

*"You are not alone and this is
not the end of your story"*

Twelve

"I didn't because I was not alone"

Background Story

Now I will tell my personal story on suicide. I grew up in a wonderful family with amazing parents. As a young boy I attended church every week with the knowledge of good and evil, heaven and hell, and the love of God. I was not only taught these things I believed them.

I remember at a very young age finding delight in reading the Bible. But when I became a teenager doubts began to weaken my belief, it seemed I was being carried away by a current of hesitations.

I Was My Own God Defining Good and Evil

Despite my strong biblical background I found myself living a hypocritical life. My introspective thoughts about God were flawed and I began to rebel. I was playing "God", defining for myself what was good and evil.

In short I was living a life that violated my divine, given purpose of knowing God. I wanted to be saved but at the same time I was ruining my own life, believing it would eventually work itself out in the end. Ultimately the time came when I stopped seeking God's opinion about how I should live.

God Getting Through to Me

At the same time unbeknown to me, God was trying to reach my heart by turning the things I deemed enjoyable into unpleasant episodes that became timeworn or as some say "they were getting old." I needed a new life; something that was more stable, something that would last for an eternity.

Issues To Being Worked Out

I recalled a story in the Bible where some thought Jesus had gone too far in *spending too much time with sinners* and eating with them. In fact, this assertion became the basis of the well-told story of the *prodigal son*. A son who had all he needed in his father's home but became disheartened with life in his fathers house and barriers to self-rule. So the son left home and encountered disaster.

At last the son came to himself and started his journey back to the father's house. I too came to myself and was convicted that I needed to return home. But I felt I had gone too far to turn around. My utmost fear came with mistaken thoughts of God leaving me because I was not worthy of His presence. In essence I felt that I was left to myself. Alone.

I could not fathom the thought that God did not want me anymore. I was a failure to Him and opportunities had now run out. There was ultimately nothing left for me but hell. I would receive no compensation for my share in this life, except living in agony without God.

For the person contemplating suicide, torturous thoughts are factors for wanting to commit suicide. We should never believe all the thoughts we have for it can be a vicious cycle. Unreliable thoughts can influence the desire to end the agonizing torture of those thoughts. Therefore, committing suicide is sadly one of bleak options.

In general any combination of emotional irreconcilable thoughts, a guilty dooming conscience, and in some cases mental illness can drive a person over the threshold of suicide.

Life Lesson Twelve: *A guilty conscience is a sign that the conscience is working and change is possible.*

I was no different. I have since understood that a *guilty conscience* is a sure sign that our conscience *is* working. That is a good thing. It is an effective application towards turning a bad situation around.

The fact is it can either work itself harmfully towards self-destruction or be the start of building healthy thoughts of purpose and hope.

If a guilty conscience is the problem then that can be restored. Having a guilty conscience is a moral issue. That is to say, it is an issue of rightness, goodness, and being honorable before God.

The only One who could have brought me to a place of rightness, goodness, and honorableness was God. I could never attain it on my own. Only God could forgive me of my wrongs, and give me the power to hate sin. But there was just one problem. I thought God did not want me. I thought God had left me. Alone.

So having access to a gun I went outside into the darkness of the night to an alleyway behind our house and sat on a galvanized trashcan to end it all. No one knew of my plan.

Somehow I needed to know
But somehow I thought to give God one more opportunity to reveal His love to me that He was still there. At that point I needed God in my life so badly that I was willing to do anything

to have His presence. If I would just accept the free gift of life offered me I would have peace.

So, I fasted and prayed to God for three days. It was the first time I had ever fasted by choice. At the conclusion of a pre-defined time for fasting I sought to discover a clear communication that God was still there and I was not alone.

The plan to know God was simple. I would turn the pages of the Bible with my eyes closed; I would then place my finger on a Bible verse. If the verse was positive then I knew God loved me, but if it was negative then I would carry out the plan to commit suicide.

This was not a good idea because it was assigning chance a role in the outcome, when what I really wanted was the sure workings of God. Besides, chance was given something it is not. Chance does not have a mind, will, or personality.

Desperate to Know

The time had arrived and I desperately needed to know that God was still with me. I felt like Job in the Bible when he said:

> "But if I go to the east, he is not there;
> if I go to the west, I do not find him.
> When he is at work in the north, I do not see him;
> when he turns to the south, I catch no glimpse of him.
> But he knows the way that I take;
> when he has tested me, I will come forth as gold. (Job 23:8-10 NIV)

So, I closed my eyes and turned the pages and placed my finger on a verse and this is what it said, *"These things have I spoken unto you, being yet present with you"* (John 14: 25).

I could not contain myself. Uncontrollable tears of joy ran down my face to the floor. I jumped in the air. I ran. I skipped. The weight of guilt was gone. The thought of suicide was vanished. Immediately I was at peace with God, the world, and myself. But more importantly I was not alone, for God was present with me.

I know this may seem like a fairy tale to some, but I open my eyes everyday enjoying life with unbelievable gratitude that I am still here by grace with purpose. Now you know why I didn't.

My appreciative optimism is that the goal of this book has been accomplished: to appeal, inspire, and serve to avoid—suicide. For I am forever grateful I didn't and I am really convinced you shouldn't, commit suicide.

Suicide Prevention Quotes

There are far, far better things ahead than anything we leave behind.

C. S. Lewis

When it is darkest, we can see the stars.

Ralph Waldo Emerson

Never let anyone else decide who you are.

Caroline Rhea

Though no one can go back and make a brand new start, anyone can start now and make a brand new ending.

Carl Bard

If your heart is still beating, God is not done with you yet.

Dillon Burroughs

Suicidal Hotlines

Need Help
Call 911
or
1-800-SUICIDE
(1-800-784-2433)
or
1-800-273-TALK
(1-800-273-8255)
or
Text Telephone:
1-800-799-4TTY
(1-800-799-4889)

Military Veterans
Suicide Hotline:
1-800-273-TALK
(Press 1)

Suicide Hotline
in Spanish:
1-800-273-TALK
(Press 2)

Reference List

Alarcon, N. (2015, February 4). *22 veterans kill themselves every day*. *CNN News*. Retrieved September 2016, from http://www.cnn.com/2015/02/04/politics/22-veterans-kill-themselves-every-day/

Albert Camus. *Stanford Encyclopedia of Philosophy* Retrieved December 2016, from https://plato.stanford.edu/entries/camus/

Ali, M. (2016). "Defeated." In defeated brainey quotes. Retrieved September 2016, from http://www.brainyquote.com/quotes/keywords/defeated.html

Baumeister, R., Crescioni, Will A., DeWall, C. Nathan, Fincham, Frank D., Lambert Nathaniel M., Stillman Tyler F., *"Alone and without purpose: Life loses meaning following social exclusion."* Retrieved December 2016, from https://www.ncbi.nlm.nih.gov/pmc/articles/PMC2717555/

Brooks, D. (2011, March 14). Ted talks. Brooks explains why there is no reason without emotion. *Huffington Post,* November 2011. Retrieved September 2016, from http://www.huffingtonpost.com/2011/03/14/ted-david-brooks_n_835476.html

Camus, A. (1955) The myth of Sisyphus and other essays. New York. Alfred A. Knopf. Random House Publishers.

Death in Hamlet. (n.d.). Chapter 3. Lesson 6. Retrieved from http://study.com/academy/lesson/death-in-hamlet.html

Fox, M. (2016, May 25). Military suicides. *NBC News*. Retrieved from http://www.nbcnews.com/health/health-news/military-suicides-most-attempts-come-soldiers-ever-see-combat-n580276

Harvey, P. (1992). *The day Philip joined the group.* Retrieved December 2016, from https://storiesforpreaching.com/philips-egg/

How Jerry Jones and Charlotte Jones made Dallas Cowboys a success. Interview. CNN video. Retrieved September 2016. http://www.today.com/video/how-jerry-jones-and-charlotte-jones-made-dallas-cowboys-a-success-688753219978

Kashdan, T. B. (2014, May 15). Why do people kill themselves: New warning signs. *Psychology Today*. Retrieved September 2016, from https://www.psychologytoday.com/blog/curious/201405/why-do-people-kill-themselves-new-warning-signs

Lanchin, M. (2012, January 24). Shoichi Yokoi, the Japanese soldier who held out in Guam. *BBC News*. Retrieved from http://www.bbc.com/news/magazine-16681636

Lorimer, G. (n.d). It's good to have money. In brainey quotes. Retrieved December 2016, from https://www.brainyquote.com/quotes/quotes/g/georgehora106813.html

Malala, J. (2013, December). Mandela looked his enemy in the eye and held him close. *World News*. Retrieved September 2016, from http://www.telegraph.co.uk/news/worldnews/

nelson-mandela/10501060/Mandela-looked-his-enemy-in-the-eye-and-held-him-close.html

Nixon, R. M. (2016). "Defeated." In defeated brainey quotes. Retrieved September 2016, from http://www.brainyquote.com/quotes/keywords/defeated.html

Orlooff, J. (2011). The health benefits of tears. Adapted from "Emotional freedom: Liberate yourself from negative emotions and transform your life." Retrieved from http://www.drjudithorloff.com/Free-Articles/The-Health-Benefits-of-Tears_copy.htm Three Rivers Press 2011

Pinkey, M., (Ed.). (2003). *The complete pocket positives.* Victoria, Australia: Five Mile Press.

Ranker Lists. (2016). Fifty-two celebrities who attempted suicide. Retrieved from http://www.ranker.com/list/celebrities-who-attempted-suicide/celebrity-lists

Remembering Elie Wiesel. (2016, July 8). Video. Retrieved from https://charlierose.com/videos/28435?autoplay=true

Rottenberg, J. (2010). Crying is not always beneficial. *Psychology Today*. Retrieved from https://www.psychologytoday.com/blog/ charting-the-depths/201007/crying-is-not-always-beneficial

Safire, W. (1997, January 26). Why do they shoot horses. *New York Times* online magazine. Retrieved from NYtimes.com

Spangler, B. (1997). *First things first.* Washington, DC: Review and Herald.

The inspiring stuff Colonel Sanders. (n.d.). Retrieved from https://www.facebook.com/TheInspiringStuff/photos/a.182766555458131.1073741829.182298638838256/190068394727947/?type=3&theater

There is a fountain filled with blood. (n.d.). Truth in history. Retrieved from http://truthinhistory.org/there-is-a-fountain-filled-with-blood.html

To be or not to be. *Wikipedia* online. Retrieved September 2016, from https://en.wikipedia.org/wiki/To_be,_or_not_to_be

vos Savant, M. (2016). "Defeated." In defeated brainey quotes. Retrieved September 2016, from http://www.brainyquote.com/quotes/ keywords/defeated.html

What are the systems in the human body. (n.d.). Retrieved September 2016, from https://www.google.com/#q=what+are+the+systems+of+the+human+body

William Cowper. (2016). *Wikipedia* online. Retrieved from https://en.wikipedia.org/wiki/William_Cowper

Zacharias, R. (2014). Ravi Zacharias on Postmodern Architect. Retrieved December 2016, from https://thelogcollege.wordpress.com/2014/01/14/ravi-zacharias-on-postmodern-architecture-at-ohio-state-university/

About the Author

Dr. Roy E. Gaiter, Sr. earned a Doctorate degree in 2014. He has served as a leader and speaker for many years in the states of Tennessee, Michigan, Florida, Mississippi, and Alabama. His experience in life as a brother to a fallen military soldier, and as a Chaplain for seven years with the Police Department has taught him compassion for families who are faced with bereavement, questioning, and healing.

Made in the USA
Middletown, DE
24 June 2019